When God made nurses He came as close to creating angels on earth as anything He ever did. Ann Gunther, R.N., is one of those special people. Tender, compassionate, this sweet Roman Catholic nursing teacher seemed to fit perfectly into God's mold as an "angel of mercy." Then something happened. Two of her three children were born deformed. Later, she and two of the children were stricken with a rare, deadly disease. For years she lived on death's threshold, fighting to hang onto what little life she had left, until— But I won't say more, for that's what this story is all about.

How Big Is God?

How Big Is God?

KATHRYN KUHLMAN

DIMENSION BOOKS
BETHANY FELLOWSHIP, INC.
Minneapolis, Minn. 55438

ISBN 0-87123-222-7

Library of Congress Catalog
Card Number 74-12775

DIMENSION BOOKS
are published by Bethany Fellowship, Inc.
6820 Auto Club Road, Minneapolis, Minnesota 55438

Printed in U.S.A.

CONTENTS

1. The Closest Thing to Job

I could feel myself falling, pitching forward down the aisle of the little chapel at St. Joseph's Infirmary in Louisville. It was a frantic, desperate feeling, as if all my muscles had melted.

A student nurse, I was in my first year of clinical training and had arrived to attend the 6:00 a.m. mass before taking my post in the infirmary. I had just stood to file up to the altar when I went limp. I tried to reach out and grab the end of a pew, but my hands had no grip. I staggered forward against the nurse in front of me, then collapsed heavily to the floor.

All the young nurses in their starchy white uniforms and caps were staring at me. One of the nuns rushed forward, grabbed me under the arms and tried to help me to my feet. But my legs were like rubber. With the help of two nurses they finally got me out into the infirmary and onto a bed in a vacant room.

"You're pushing yourself too hard, Ann," one of the doctors said after my strength had returned. "I'm going to keep you in bed for a few days so you can rest."

When I was a little girl of thirteen, Mother had enrolled me in a Saturday morning ballet class in Louisville. Even way back then I tired easily. I could seldom get through an entire dancing session. My legs would just stop working, and I would have to sit down while the other girls performed their *arabesques, jetes,* and *pirouettes.*

Mom took me to a doctor in our suburb of Shively, outside of Louisville. He noticed I also had double vision and sent me to an eye doctor who made a thorough examination. The eye doctor couldn't find any occular problems and advised Mom to take me to a neurologist. However, back in 1945 a neurologist was hard to find, so the matter was dropped. Besides, the condition seemed to come and go. For a few weeks I would be fine, then the exhaustion would return—along with the double vision and shortness of breath.

It was springtime and I had been chosen to sing a solo for the recital put on by the school of ballet. Mother had me practicing all afternoon, but I noticed the more I sang the more my voice seemed to fade away. That night all the girls were on stage, dressed in their pretty ballet costumes. The auditorium was filled with admiring parents, relatives and friends. But when I stepped forward to sing my solo, nothing came out. I mean I opened my mouth to sing but there was no sound. The muscles in my throat simply would not function. The piano played on and I mouthed the words with my lips, but there was nothing. I broke into tears and ran from the

11

stage, hiding in the wings in a little dressing room. The shame of the moment, the embarrassment of having let my parents down, was too much for me.

It was the first time I had heard those words which I would hear so many times over the following years, this time coming from forgiving parents. "You're just overworked, Ann. Get some rest and you'll be all right."

Rest helped. In fact, it became a necessary element in my life. Other children could take part in athletics or go out for cheerleader, but my time was spent confined to my room after school, resting and studying. I wanted to be a nurse— the finest nurse in the world. Thanks to a full scholarship to Nazareth College I was able to concentrate on getting my degree in nursing. But physical activity was out. My body just would not stand the strain of exercise.

One morning I was climbing the stairs to a third floor chemistry lab when I collapsed. I didn't faint; my muscles just refused to hold me up. I knew everything that was going on, each rolling fall, each jarring bump until I landed in a heap on the landing of the stairs.

I was ordered to remain in bed all that day and a doctor gave me a physical examination. Again I heard the words, "You're working too hard. You're physically exhausted. You need to slow down."

I spent most of the next six months in bed, slowly regaining my strength. I was finally able to return to nursing school and graduate with honors.

By the time I got to my clinical work at St. Joseph's Hospital, physical exhaustion had become a way of life for me. My last year there I married, but this only increased my problems. Thirty-seven months after the birth of my first child, I found myself with two more babies (the two youngest born with severe birth defects) and a husband who because of chronic physical, emotional and spiritual illness could no longer cope with or be expected to help with rearing our family.

Joey, our middle child, was baptized in the nursery of the hospital by a nurse because the doctors did not expect him to live. Denied oxygen at birth because of a horrible cleft palate, he had also suffered brain damage. Yet he lived. I had to feed him with a lamb's nipple or a medicine dropper for the first several months of his life. He had no palate at all and no gums on one side. Besides this, he couldn't drink milk or milk substitutes, was covered with rashes, was underweight and couldn't retain food. The allergist found 105 things his body could not tolerate. I had to prepare a liquid from mashed potatoes, which meant coming home each day after work, mashing this mush so it would go through a lamb's nipple, and then spending another two hours trying to feed him.

Then Ronnie was born with a cleft lip. We started into a long series of plastic surgery operations—first on Joey to restore his mouth, nose and face, and then on Ronnie. Joey's condition was most severe, however, for the doctors confirmed he not only had brain damage but was permanently deaf in one ear with minimal hearing in the other.

The year after Ronnie was born, my discouraged husband left us. This was indeed painful.

One of the priests, where I was working at the time, told me, "Ann, you are the closest thing to Job I know in this modern generation."

2. I Have Myasthenia Gravis

The doctors conceded that the birth defects could have been caused by my exposure to X rays. Prior to Joey's birth, while I was carrying him, I would return to my nursing position as often as I could, even if for only a few weeks at a time. I desperately needed the money. However, during this time I spent much time in the X-ray department, and the overexposure to the radiation had taken its grim toll.

For several years I was head nurse

at Our Lady of Peace, a psychiatric hospital in Louisville. Later I took a teaching position at St. Mary's School of Nursing. The job was perfect for me. I didn't have the long hours on my feet and was assigned a position as an instructor in medical nursing, teaching young nurses, in particular, how to act when they encounter death. Many nurses become hardened by death. Others become tender and loving. I was anxious for my students to develop a tender nature, for one day they would become God's instruments to comfort people in their time of greatest need.

But the satisfaction of the new job did not help my physical condition. More and more I was having times of "total weakness" when my muscles stopped working. The "attacks" would last only a few minutes and then I would revive. But I was steadily growing weaker and weaker.

Finally my supervisor took a hand. I had returned one afternoon to my office. She waited until I was at my desk before she entered.

"I just saw you come down the hall,"

she said with a concerned look on her face. "You could hardly walk from that classroom to your office."

I leaned my head heavily in my hands. There was no sense trying to ignore the facts any longer. Something was wrong. I knew it.

"I don't believe that you are simply run down," she said. "There is something wrong with your muscles. I want you to see a neurologist."

The doctor was a young neurologist who had just come from residency. He was up-to-date on all the new discoveries in medicine and I felt secure in his care. I spent considerable time with him on my first appointment as he thoroughly reviewed my medical record and gave me a complete physical examination. Then he gave me some pills to "pep me up."

"Call me tomorrow afternoon," he said definitely. "I want to know how you feel after taking this medicine."

The next afternoon I was feeling worse than ever. I wasn't even able to go to work. I called the doctor from the house. "I feel much worse," I complained.

"I suspected as much," he said, showing no alarm. "Now take the second bottle of pills I gave you."

That evening, after taking the other little white tablets, I really felt better—fast. I knew then what he was doing. He had set me up on the first medication to rule out fatigue from abnormal stress.

The following day I returned to his office. He told me I would have to come back once a week until he could regulate the new medication. "It has rather potent side effects," he said cautiously. I asked no more questions. He told me to take the pills once every thirty minutes during my waking hours, warning me he might have to increase the dosage to once every fifteen minutes. I knew too many nurses who picked up fancied symptoms from the patients, jumping to all kinds of false conclusions. Just having a doctor who seemed to know what he was doing, and who was bringing a measure of relief, was enough for me. I was determined to be a good patient, ask no questions, and take my medicine as ordered.

Well, that attitude lasted about two

weeks. My medical curiosity was boiling inside. It was a Tuesday afternoon. I was in the medical library at St. Mary's preparing a lecture for the next morning when I saw some neurological medical books which had been pulled from the stacks and left on the table. I knew I had a muscle condition which responded to drugs. I had also quizzed the hospital pharmacist and knew the name of the drug. With the help of the books and the latest medical journals, I discovered there was only one kind of neurological condition that responded to this particular medication—myasthenia gravis.

That night after the children were in bed, I went back to my nursing school notes on neurology. I found a small paragraph dealing with myasthenia gravis, a rare, progressive disease. In my own handwriting, scribbled at the bottom of the page, were the words: "Patients usually die within two years. No hope. Incurable."

I sat at the little table in my kitchen, the notes spread out in front of me. There was no panic. I had been sick too long for this to catch me unawares. Over and over I thought of the lectures I had given my students, telling them how to prepare people for death.

"Life at its best is only a vapor," I had told them, quoting from the Bible. "No doctor, no priest, understands how life is created. It is a gift of God, breathed into a fertilized egg, nourished by the mother's bloodstream, brought into this world by the miracle of birth, loved by parents, trained by others who have gone before, used of God to create other lives, and finally, in the same mysterious process by which it was given, it is taken away. The Lord gives. The Lord takes away."

I sat at the little table. The house was quiet with only the hushed swish-swish of the leaves from an old tree brushing gently against the windowpane. I nodded in silent recognition and murmured the rest of that ancient quote from Job, "Blessed be the name of the Lord."

I thought of Daddy. He had died suddenly one Sunday night at the age of fifty-four. For several years he had been in declining health—weakness, fatigue.

He, too, had been under the care of a neurologist. But then one night, after he and mother had spent a quiet day together, he dropped to the floor and died. The doctors were mystified. They never did find out what killed him.

The next morning I returned to the medical books. I wanted to learn everything I could about this killer that had invaded my life. Myasthenia gravis is an electrical breakdown in the nervous system of the body. Every move of every muscle is controlled by an impulse from the brain which runs down a nerve much as an electrical current runs down a copper wire. This electrical (nervous) impulse is transmitted to the muscles through a chemical known as acetylcholine.

In myasthenia gravis there is an imbalance in this chemical. When fatigue occurs the nerves gradually cease to send this juice over to the muscles so they can flex. All the generalized voluntary muscles in the body are affected: the muscles in the throat (how vividly I remembered that pantomime solo at the ballet concert), the eyelids, swallowing, and worst of all, the lungs. Without a respirator you cannot breathe, for your lungs refuse to inhale air. You die within minutes.

Perhaps that is what happened to my father, I thought. Mother said he had just "gasped for breath" and died. Four of his brothers had died in infancy of "crib death"—that mysterious disease which has no known cause. Since the cause of myasthenia gravis is in the chemical transmission at the time, this would not even show up in an autopsy, for there is no pathology in the muscle itself. That is why the disease is so difficult to diagnose and treat.

Further reading revealed that some forms of myasthenia gravis are passed on from parent to child—for several generations. I shuddered, thinking of my three children at home.

3. Hoping Against Hope

Carol, now four years old, didn't seem to play normally. She tired easily, complained of weakness and whined because she was so exhausted. Surely, what had killed my father, and was now killing me, wouldn't be passed on to Carol also. Yet . . .

That afternoon I was back in the doctor's office. "You don't have to tell me what you suspect," I said. "I already know."

He motioned me to a chair. Then half-sitting on the corner of his desk, fiddling with his stethoscope dangling from his neck, he looked straight into my face.

"Okay, you're a nurse. You know that a diagnosis is very difficult at this point. It is important that you not be discouraged. Whether this is myasthenia gravis or not, at least we're bringing it under some kind of control."

I wasn't discouraged. I just figured it was another cross for me to carry.

I took the medication for six months, and it provided enough relief so I could work and take care of the children. A woman had moved in with us as a live-in housekeeper, which helped considerably. It also enabled me to do something I had put off for several years— begin a Saturday morning course at Spalding College in Louisville, working toward a master's degree in nursing. This was partly the doctor's idea for "supportive therapy," partly out of my own financial need to improve my pay scale by getting the graduate degree.

Of course with my work load during the day and caring for the children at night, I had almost no time to study. The night before the final exam—the night I had set aside to cram—all three of the children were sick. I went into the class the next day with almost no sleep and having done less preparation. I needed the credit to complete my degree, which in turn would increase my salary. It looked as if I were doomed to failure.

The professor, who prided himself on being a tricky test-giver, made a little speech before he passed out the exam. He told us it was impossible to make a perfect score on the test. Even the hospital administrators who were working in the field had never made a perfect score.

I bowed my head in despair. A prayer the nuns had taught me when I was a little girl came to mind. I gave it silent voice.

"Come, Holy Spirit, fill the hearts of Thy faithful, and enkindle in them the fire of Your love. Send forth Your Spirit and let them be recreated, and Thou wilt renew the face of the earth."

Then I added my own P.S. "I know You are the source of all enlightenment and You know my needs."

I made the only perfect score in the history of the class.

Six months later the old symptoms began to return. This was cause for hope. My medicine was useless *unless* I had myasthenia gravis. If I had the disease, the medicine would give me strength. If I did not have it, it would have no value.

I called the doctor. "The medicine's not working any more. Perhaps I don't have myasthenia gravis," I said happily.

"Do you have any kind of infection?" he asked.

I admitted I had a bad cold. He then told me the medicine does not always work in the presence of an infection. This could mean I might have to be put in a respirator in case my lungs ceased to function.

I felt panic building up inside me. I had seen polio patients in the hospital whose lungs were paralyzed. The only way they could breathe was to be placed in an iron lung, or strapped to a positive respirator that pumped their lungs, forcing them to inhale and exhale. In fact, I had seen patients die because they could not get air. It was a horrible death.

Sensing my near panic, the doctor suggested it was time to have his diagnosis confirmed by another physician. He mentioned a physician in Indianapolis, a specialist in myasthenia gravis.

I had heard of this man, although the circumstances had been depressing. A nursing colleague had told me about the Myasthenia Gravis Foundation in New York City. Wondering if there might be anyone else in Kentucky who had this rare disease, I wrote to the Foundation.

One evening, three weeks later, there was a knock at the door of our home in Valley Station. A man who lived only a short distance from my house had received my name from the Foundation. His wife also had MG. We became friends and I learned her physician was the specialist in Indianapolis.

That spring she had a crisis. Her lungs stopped working. Her husband put her in the car and tried to get her to the doctor, but it was too late. She died at the age of 32.

I was bitter toward God; and for the first time, fearful. Was this to be my fate also? I didn't want to die. Who would care for my three babies?

"You wouldn't do that to me, would You, God?" I pleaded. But deep inside I didn't believe it was God who had caused me to be sick. My real fears were that God was too far away to be able to help me.

Grasping at straws, and hoping against hope that I did not have MG, I made an appointment with the doctor in Indianapolis. It took only a few moments in his office before I understood why the other physicians described him as an expert. After carefully checking my medical records, he strapped me in a special chair—a chair that had electrical connections that ran to a graph machine. Much as an EKG measures impulses from the heart, this chair measures the strength of the muscles of the body. When I leaned backwards it recorded my back muscles. When I squeezed a little ball it measured the muscle strength in my hands and fingers. Chin muscles were tested by raising my head.

Next came two hypodermics. I had read up on the procedure and knew what was coming. I would receive two hypos several minutes apart. One of them would be a placebo, a shot of water in the vein. If I had MG this would cause no change in the ergo-graph. The other would contain a special drug, *tensilon*, designed to give temporary relief to a myasthenic, but it would not affect an ordinary person. When I received that hypo the graph would react radically because of my new strength.

Of course, I did not know which hypo was the water and which was the tensilon. But the doctor did, and the ergograph recorded it. I definitely had myasthenia gravis.

4. The First Crisis

The doctor asked me to follow him into his office where he calculated my responses from the graph and regulated my medication. He then told me what to expect in the future. Infections, even minor ones, would put me to bed for weeks. He cautioned me not to fight my condition, saying I would live longer if I didn't panic when I went into a crisis.

"Is it right that I have only a couple of years to live?" I asked.

"You're a nurse, Mrs. Gunther," he

said gently. "And you're a teacher of nurses. Therefore I am going to talk straight."

He reached out and touched my elbow, guiding me to a chair in his office. Taking a seat behind his desk, he pulled off his glasses and leaned forward. "No doctor has the right," he said in a soft voice, "to limit your life like that. Besides, there are several categories of myasthenia gravis. The brittle myasthenic might live as long as two years before he goes into a crisis. The intermediate myasthenic could live ten or fifteen years if his medicine is regulated properly. It all depends on how many times you experience a crisis condition in which your lungs fail and you have to go into a respirator. Your heart can stand only so much strain, and life expectancy isn't good after two major crises."

He then told me I fit into a "borderline brittle" category. In other words, my days were numbered.

The doctor was right about expecting the crises. They started soon afterwards, building in intensity. The first one came soon after I returned from Indianapolis. I couldn't get my medicine regulated. In the beginning I was taking one pill every fifteen minutes, which meant I always had to carry a full supply with me wherever I went. To leave the house without my medicine could mean death on the sidewalk. To forget and take too many pills could send me into a spasm similar to that which soldiers exposed to poison gas might experience on a battlefield. It seemed as if every waking second was spent struggling to stay alive.

My first major crisis occurred one night away from home. I had become active in the local MG Foundation and had been invited to speak to a group of people at the mall on Shelbyville Road. I seldom went out at night, usually being in bed by eight o'clock. My eyes were bad, and sometimes I would see four headlights rather than two. Glasses were no good, so I had stopped driving except during the daylight hours.

It was a rainy night in June. Lois, one of the nurses at St. Joseph's Hospital, had picked me up for the meeting and was now driving me home. The stately poplars that lined the dark streets were hidden by the pelting rain which beat against the windshield like scattered shot. I leaned back in the seat beside her, listening to the steady whoosh-whoosh of the windshield wipers. How tired I felt. The car seemed awfully warm and it was hard to breathe. Suddenly I realized my lungs were not working. When I tried to inhale nothing happened. Only by opening my mouth and swallowing desperately could I force air into my lungs. I was suffocating!

I groped out and felt Lois' arm, afraid to move my head from its locked position. My mouth stretched open, gasping, trying to suck in air. She had already noticed. She had heard the horrible sucking noise coming from my throat.

Jamming the car in gear, she swerved around two cars waiting for a red light and with horn blowing, headed toward the emergency room at St. Joseph's. The beat of the windshield wipers syncopated with my wild gasping for breath. Over and over I repeated the doctor's words in my mind. "Don't panic. Relax. Don't fight it." But when your body is starving for air, panic is only a blink away. I knew my bloodstream was being deprived of life-giving oxygen. I was dying.

Skidding on the dark, wet streets, Lois finally pulled into the lighted portico outside St. Joseph's. Moments later two male attendants were lifting me onto a stretcher and bursting through the doors. I could feel the wheels bumping along the uneven floor as they raced me into a cubical where a positive respirator was strapped around my chest and face. I felt the machine begin to lift my body at regular intervals, pumping air into my lungs. I gulped it readily.

Two nurses were working, massaging my hands and feet. "Her nails are blue," I heard one of them say. I wanted to talk, to tell them I was alive, but the mask over my mouth and nose kept me silent. I looked up into the face of a strange doctor. He was adjusting the machine which was pumping my chest, causing my lungs to expand and contract mechanically. A needle was in my arm and I felt my body relax. Gradually my lungs were beginning to work again on their own—inhale, exhale, inhale, exhale. Never before had I realized how much I took my lungs for granted.

"Take her up to ICU [Intensive Care Unit]," the doctor said. "We'll keep her on the respirator all night. Keep the injections going every thirty minutes. I think she's going to make it."

The room was swimming before my eyes. I tried to think of the children. It was Ronnie's fifth birthday. He would be terrified when I did not return home. But my mind refused to focus. I knew I was being moved along the corridor on the stretcher. Attendants on each side were supporting the IV bottles and the respirator equipment. It was the same role played every day as I wheeled patients to and from their assigned places. Now the cast of characters had changed. I was on the bed, gasping for life, and others were ministering to me. A nun, her sweet face encased in her black and white habit, bent over me as I was entering ICU. I saw her lips moving in prayer. I tried to reach out and touch her in love, but my arm was held in place by the tubes. All I could do was try to say "thank you" with my eyes. I felt her cool hand on my head and then I was in the ICU room. The night disappeared into the fog.

It was a week before I was released from the hospital. The doctor explained I had a viral infection and a low grade fever which had conteracted the medicine, making it virtually ineffective. Not aware of how serious any infection could be, I had allowed myself to become fatigued. The chemicals which carried the involuntary messages from my nerves to my muscles had stopped working.

"Muscles," said the doctor the day he dismissed me from the hospital, "work only because the brain tells them to work. When the message doesn't get through because of a faulty connection, they don't do anything. Your lungs stopped getting messages to inhale and exhale. Like any piece of machinery that is no longer being told what to do, they just ceased functioning until the messages were restored. If this happens and there is no respirator or iron lung close by, you'll quickly die of suffocation, or your heart will fail."

"What if I'm home alone when it happens?" I asked, feeling desperately helpless.

He repeated the specialist's advice: "Don't panic. Relax. Your brain is functioning normally and will keep shooting impulses to the lungs. If you relax, some of them will get through. But if you fight it, the chemical reaction will be negative and you'll be gone."

The night after I got home, I gathered the children around me. In simple words I tried to explain that at any time I might have another crisis. I would need their help.

"I'll phone the doctor," Carol said.

"And I'll remind you to take your pills," little Ronnie chimed.

Joey, struggling with his words, reached out and took my hand. "I'll hold your hand, Mommy, so you won't be afraid."

Joey knew what fear was, but he knew nothing of the fear of suffocating. "Don't panic." The words ran over and over in my mind. But how can you keep from going into a panic when you can't breathe? Only God could help me now.

The four of us held hands. "Children,

I need your prayers," I said, trying to hold back the tears. Then speaking to God I said, "Lord, without You we are lost."

The house was silent. But in my heart I felt peace. God was there, listening.

5. Overdose!

The medicine held the disease in check. But there was always the danger I would forget to take it. This meant if I went out of the house, even into the yard, without my pills, I might never make it back inside.

One afternoon a friend stopped by to take me shopping. It was a stupid thing, but I didn't check my little pill box to see how many I had inside. When we parked in the parking lot of the shopping center, I decided to take a pill before getting out of the car. I opened the box and it was empty. I had taken my last pill just before my friend arrived. I had meant to refill the box, but had been interrupted by the doorbell and had forgotten. Now here we were, thirty minutes from the house, with no medication.

I remained in the car while she ran to a nearby Walgreen's. The druggist called the doctor and found out what he had been giving me. From then on I carried a locket around my neck that held a pill for just such emergencies.

But my condition gradually deteriorated. My weight was down to ninety-eight pounds. It seemed my body was building up resistance to the drugs. The doctors in Louisville recommended cobalt treatment. Had the disease been diagnosed earlier they might have tried surgery. But it had progressed too far. So the doctors began cobalt treatment on my thymus gland.

Every day, for three months, I entered the hospital for the radiation treatment. My neck was marked with a big purple pencil and each morning, for a split second, the technician would send deep X rays into my thymus. Within a week my body began to swell and I turned puffy all over—bloated. The inside of my mouth was sore from the effects of the radiation. The skin on my neck was burned and began to wrinkle. At the same time I was horribly nauseated. Yet the doctors felt that even though the outcome was uncertain, it was better to try the X ray than to sit around doing nothing.

It was a year later when I had my first cholinergic crisis, caused from an overdose of the medication. The doctors had warned me that too much of the medicine would kill me even quicker than not enough.

I had stayed home from work that day because the children were sick. They were always sick, it seemed. And I had a splitting headache. I knew I shouldn't take any other medication as long as I was taking my doctor's prescription, but the head pain was so great I thought I would chance a couple of aspirins. I was in the kitchen and had just taken two of my own pills when I realized that instead of taking two aspirins, I had mistakenly taken two more pills.

Immediately my mouth began to fill with saliva. My stomach and intestines were cramping. My eyes felt like the sockets were just there—but no eyeballs. My vision went out of proportion. All in moments.

Carol heard me cry out and ran to me. I had collapsed on the kitchen floor.

"Call the doctor," I stammered.

"Oh, my goodness!" he said when I told him what was happening. "How long ago did you overdose."

"About 15 minutes ago," I said, my mouth now frothing furiously.

"You've got about fifteen minutes left," he said. "Take the atropine immediately."

Atropine was an antidote which I kept on hand in case of an overdose. It is the same antidote used against the curare poison which South American Indians use to tip their arrows. In fact, a cholinergic crisis is very similar to the effects of the curare poison.

The doctor told me how much of the antidote to take, and Carol prepared the hypodermic as I lay on the kitchen floor. I managed to get the needle into the top of my leg. The doctor was still on the telephone. "If the conditions don't subside in ten minutes," he said, "get to the emergency room immediately."

I lay back on the floor, my head in Carol's lap, and prayed. The conditions did begin to subside. The cramping eased and the saliva in my mouth stopped running. I knew I could help things by wearing the drug out of my system, so I began to crawl. I dragged myself on my knees all over the house, using up the extra chemical I had put into my body. Carol crawled with me, holding up my head which dangled uselessly. Gradually my body returned to its former state. I determined that night never to take another aspirin. Better to suffer the pain of a headache than run the risk of a cholinergic crisis.

6. The Final Blow!

The worst, though, was yet to come. As horrible as myasthenia gravis was, at least I could face it. But when it became evident that Carol might have something wrong with her, I almost went to pieces. Of course I had known, as far back as Carol's early childhood, that she wasn't able to play normally. I took her regularly to the pediatrician, but he seemed to think she was only mimicking my symptoms. The neurologist, on the other hand, warned me when Carol entered the first grade that there was a possibility she might have some form of myasthenia gravis—a thought which so horrified me I completely blanked it out of my mind.

Yet as Carol grew older it became very evident she was showing the same symptoms I had shown as a child. Although she was a bright child, she fatigued easily. Then one day in the first grade her teacher phoned me from the Catholic school she was attending.

"Carol seems to be working too hard," she said. "Perhaps she isn't getting enough rest at home."

"Oh, no," I replied, trying to act calmly. "She goes to bed very early in the evening."

"Well, something is wrong," the teacher continued. "Even though she is a smart child, she can't seem to stay awake. This afternoon she just fell over on her desk, she was so tired."

After receiving several other phone calls from the school, and on two occasions having to go get her and bring her home, I took her to the neurologist. He put her on three pills a day—a heavy dosage for a little girl—and recommended I have her tested. I went home and cried all night that time. Was she going to have to face the same thing I had faced all my life? Was God so distant that He was unable to help even a child?

Our financial condition was desperate also. Unable to work much of the time, I was having to fall back on seeking some disability benefits. It was difficult for a myasthenic to get social security benefits unless he was going through a crisis when examined by a doctor. Fortunately, my doctors knew my condition and my social security went through—total disability.

It was one of those straws that I was grasping for as I went under—only this straw helped keep me afloat. Every day on the job had become more difficult. I couldn't climb steps any more. I couldn't even use my hands to pump up a blood pressure cuff on a patient's arm. Staying home with the children at least helped me to cope with my illness, as well as take care of them. The social security benefits also gave me enough money to take Carol to Indianapolis for an appointment with the specialist.

I stayed with her while he ran the tests —the same ones he had run on me.

"This little girl has really had fortitude to exist with this," he said.

"You mean it is myasthenia gravis?" I moaned, my voice ready to break.

He nodded. "I don't like to call it hereditary, because it is not like diabetes where you can predict a definite path. I prefer to call it a recurring type. In this case we've detected it in the early stages, and if she takes the proper dosage of *mesteinon* she should do well. I doubt if there will be any real problems before she reaches puberty. Then . . ." He paused and chewed his lip. "Well, we'll have to wait and see."

He went ahead to say the Myasthenia Gravis Foundation was constantly raising money for research and maybe by the time Carol was twelve years old, they would have discovered a new drug. But I wasn't able to hear him. I had turned away to hide the tears. It just wasn't fair. First Daddy. Then me. Now Carol. When would this horrible chain be broken?

The black night of my soul was to grow even darker, however. Three years later, after having gone through crisis after crisis, after having collapsed on the city streets and having been rushed to the hospital by strangers, after having been in and out of respirators and iron lungs, after having gone through thirteen operations with Joey and receiving the news he would always be totally deaf in his left ear from a defective nerve, after having lived in the suburbs of hell and on the threshold of death, with only the thought of my children needing me to keep me alive, I received the final blow. It came during a parent-teacher conference with Ronnie's first-grade teacher.

"He's a smart little boy," she said, "but he has the worst time writing. His eyes droop. Is he getting enough sleep?"

"Oh dear God!" I gasped. "This can't be so. Please don't let it be so."

But it was so. The doctor confirmed it. Ronnie had myasthenia.

So there we were. Carol and Ronnie confirmed with a chronic disease and poor Joey, struggling along with his deaf ear and more perceptual handicaps than

I can list. He was just dragging along in his special education classes at school. At least the other children had strong minds, but despite how hard Joey struggled in school, he fell farther and farther behind. We huddled together, like children lost in the woods, barely surviving on a day-by-day basis.

Yet it was in this huddling together as a family that we learned to pray together. Ronnie was determined to go into the Lord's work, perhaps as a Franciscan priest. Despite the fact we were all dying—slowly, by degrees—there was a spark of life kindling in our souls. Spiritual life.

One day a friend said, "Look, we hear there are miracles happening in Pittsburgh. People are healed of incredible illnesses at miracle services conducted by Kathryn Kuhlman.

This didn't shock me. As a Roman Catholic I had heard of miracles as long ago as I could remember. I had read of healing at Lourdes, France, and at St. Anne's in Quebec, Canada. But this was so far away. And never having seen a miracle, nor having known anyone who had received one, I was skeptical.

Besides, I had become extremely active in the Myasthenia Gravis Foundation, and was now the coordinator for the Foundation in the State of Kentucky. Besides traveling throughout the state speaking about the work of the Foundation, I felt responsible to help with patient encouragement. Whenever I received word of a newly diagnosed case of myasthenia gravis in our area, I would be on the phone, encouraging, reassuring. So, even though I was suffering, I found some meaning in the life I had left by serving through the Foundation. Of course I strongly believed that one day there would be a medical research breakthrough and a cure would be discovered. That hope, however, dulled my desperation—my willingness to look for a miracle—and did nothing to ease the present state of my disease. I needed a hope far greater than that.

Then two things happened which changed my mind. The first almost cost me my life. The second gave me life.

7. At the Arie Crown Theatre

Spring was early that year. The dogwoods were in full bloom, their white and pink petals had transformed Louisville into a fairy wonderland. The red azaleas were bursting into bloom at every corner, and the city seemed alive with color.

I had fixed the children's supper. Ronnie had just gotten out of the hospital following a crisis at school. He was now home in bed and Carol and Joey were helping me with the supper dishes. I leaned against the sink, so tired. I started to ask Carol to hand me a dish towel when I felt it happening. My lungs were closing down. The doctor's words flashed through my mind. *"Life expectancy isn't good after two major crises."* I had been through many more than that. Now this one, which seemed so different as it swept over my body. I had an ominous feeling, a feeling of doom as I slumped to the floor. I desperately motioned for Carol to call a neighbor on the phone. Within minutes I was in her car, speeding toward the hospital.

This time, though, something told me I'd never make it. I was dying. A police car was behind us, siren wailing and blue light flashing. I was aware of our car stopping, bouncing along the gravel on the shoulder of the road. My mind was in total alert, but my body—my lungs in particular—had stopped living. Strong hands picked me up and put me in the back seat of the squad car. I felt the oxygen mask go over my face, but I couldn't inhale. My chest muscles had stopped working.

Oddly, I never lost consciousness. I could hear, smell, think—but I could not move. I heard a familiar voice. It was a nurse at St. Joseph's.

"Oh God, she's dying," she said softly. "Her feet are like ice."

I was in the emergency room. Another nurse had my hands. "She's comatose," she said with a touch of panic in her voice. "Get her on positive pressure therapy."

I felt the respirator begin to work. A doctor lifted my eyelids, but like all the other muscles in my body, my eyes were disconnected from my nervous system. Except for a faint heartbeat, I showed every evidence of being dead.

Doctors and nurses were working feverishly now. I could hear their conversation over me, every word, although they thought I was already gone.

"Better send for Father Brennan," I heard the voice of the head nurse. The loudspeaker was paging the chaplain, telling him to rush to emergency.

I was dying—yet I felt great peace. In my heart I said, "Oh, Jesus, I just turn it all over to You."

Dying was nothing like I thought it would be. I was not even anxious about my children. They, too, were in God's hands. Faith comes in full force at vital times.

I lived. Transferred to ICU, I remained in the hospital for ten days and then was sent home. I was not the same, though. Dying changes something inside a person. For the first time I was ready for a miracle.

Nell Adams was a member of the Myasthenia Gravis Foundation. She had been putting constant pressure on me for years.

"I know God heals," she kept saying. "I know miracles happen. I've been healed. If God can do it for a member of the Unity church like me, He can certainly do it for a Roman Catholic."

I remained polite, but distant. She knew she wasn't getting through to me, even when she testified of having been healed in a Kathryn Kuhlman miracle service in Pittsburgh. But after this last crisis, I was ready to listen.

"Ann," she said gently, "you're just hard-headed. You're going all over the state informing people about myasthenia gravis. Wouldn't it be wonderful if you could also tell them about the power of God to heal one who has the disease?"

I was listening. I knew I'd never live through another crisis.

Then something else happened. A nurse called me to the phone and told me about an interdenominational meeting—she called it a charismatic conference—to be held at Christ's Church Cathedral in downtown Louisville. I knew of Christ's Church. The Episcopalians had been very generous in letting us use their building for MG Foundation meetings. The nurse told me about the wonderful meeting she had attended that morning when Christians from all churches had come together to praise the Lord.

"These people all believe God can heal the sick," she said. "Maybe you should go and see if anything happens."

I did go. I sat near the back of the great stone cathedral. The man next to me introduced himself as a Baptist preacher. I looked around and saw sev-

Kathryn Kuhlman ministering at the Houston Coliseum, Houston, Texas Photo by Doug Granstaff

61

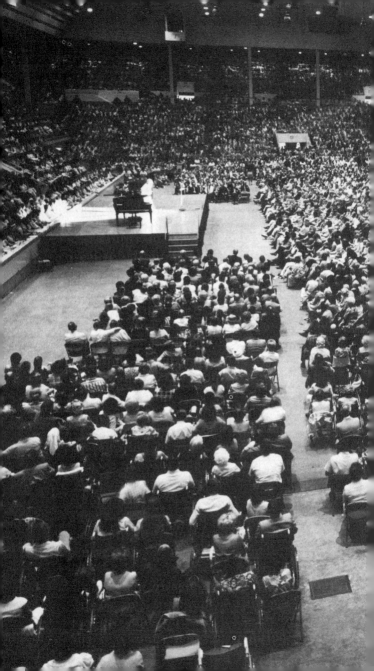

eral people I knew. My, how these people sang! They praised God vocally, too. The woman in front of me, whom I had met at a cursillo at St. Boniface Catholic Church several years before, held her hands above her head as she sang.

But this was not for me. I was so tired. I had to sit down. Yet at the close when the speaker had us all join hands and repeat the "Our Father" together, something sparked inside me. A Catholic nurse and a Baptist preacher holding hands and praying together; maybe this was for real. That night I decided to call Nell Adams and talk to her about Kathryn Kuhlman.

Instead of Pittsburgh, however, we would be going to Chicago. It seemed Miss Kuhlman was to be speaking at the Arie Crown Theatre and a chartered bus was going from Louisville. By taking the bus we could be assured of seats.

I took all three children, thinking perhaps one of them might be healed even if I wasn't. The people on the bus were friendly, helping each other as we got off and entered the huge auditorium near

Lake Michigan. There were 11,000 present, and we were given seats in the balcony.

The meeting began with singing, and it was impossible to keep from joining in. I looked down the row at the children. They, too, were singing with enthusiasm.

I knew it was real. All those people praising God—how could anything but good come out of such a meeting? After Miss Kuhlman spoke she began to identify people who were being healed. All over the auditorium people were standing to their feet to claim particular healings. But in the middle of it all I got deathly nauseated and began to ache all over.

"I had better get to the Ladies' Room," I whispered to Carol. "I'm sick to my stomach."

I staggered down the stairs to the main floor, but as suddenly as it appeared, the nausea stopped. I was feeling normal again.

"Well, I've gotten this far," I thought. "I'm going down where I can see the platform from the side." I wanted to see, close up, those who said they had been healed.

I stood in the shadows and watched them. Some cases could be explained as psychosomatic. But others were definite healings. I began praying for my children—especially for Joey who had been through so much.

"Lord, more than anything else in all the world I want to see my children well."

But nothing happened, and I made my way back to my seat. Perhaps God was too busy with all these others to hear my simple, unworthy plea. I looked at Joey, his eyes darting here and there as his mind tried to grasp what was going on.

"Please God, please!" I sobbed inwardly as I slumped back in my seat. "Not me. Just Joey."

Then the meeting was over, and we were being rushed to our bus.

8. An Uncapped Spring

The children were restless, exhausted. I was in pain. We rode all night and I stumbled into the house the next day saying bitterly to Nell, "It was a mistake. If we had gone into a crisis on the bus, we'd be dead. I'll never do it again."

Withdrawing from any hope of being healed at a miracle service did not mean, however, that I had withdrawn from God. Quite the opposite. As spring flowed into summer our family began, for the first time, to be drawn together as one spiritual unit.

For years I had kept a big, beautiful Bible on the coffee table in the living room. It was there, of course, to give the impression we were religious people. But after our return from Chicago things changed spiritually.

It began at supper the night following. Carol was full of questions about what we had seen and heard at the meeting, especially the miracles. We all knew that God performed miracles. After all, that was His business. If He created the world, He certainly had the right—and the power—to make any changes He desired, even instantaneous changes. We believed such changes often came about through prayer. But it was quite another thing to believe God might perform a miracle on us.

The conversation at the table grew lively and moments later Ronnie went into the living room and returned with the Bible. "Instead of arguing with each other," he said, with a wisdom far beyond his 12 years, "let's see what God has to say about all this." With that he plopped the Bible in front of me.

"Yeah, Mom," Joey chimed in.

"Aren't you supposed to be our leader? Tell us what the Bible has to say."

Even though I had been a believer for years, I had little knowledge of the Bible. Perhaps because it was "holy," I had been afraid to touch it—to get familiar with it. Or maybe it was the King James English with all the "thees" and "thous" that made me shy away. Whatever it was, now I was being challenged by my children to tell them what God had to say about miracles and healings, and the only place I could find my information was in the Bible.

We were at the table for more than two hours that night. My first efforts to find passages in the Bible were pretty stumbling, but as the days flew by I became more and more familiar with the simple stories of Jesus, the letters of Paul, and those marvelous events recorded in the book of Acts. Sometimes we would sit down to watch television and one of the children would say, "Why do we have to watch this junk? Let's read the Bible."

"Yeah, yeah," the others would join in. So off went the TV and out came the Bible. Sometimes I would read it, sometimes Carol or Ronnie. Joey, who was struggling with his reading, would be content to interrupt the rest of us by asking questions.

"Hey, don't read so fast. If Jesus could cast demons out of people back then, and told His followers to do it also, why can't we?"

This would raise a whole new series of questions about demons, and whether man had dominion over them. The Bible would be passed from hand to hand as each of us thought about places where we might find more information.

Then one night we stumbled into Paul's first letter to the church at Corinth. We began reading about the Holy Spirit and the gifts He brings with Him—miracles, healings, prophecies, tongues. It was a whole new world we had discovered.

"Say, Mom," Ronnie said, "here it's been all the time. God wants to fill us with His Holy Spirit. See," he said, pointing to I Corinthians 12 and then flipping back to various chapters in the book of Acts, "God wants us to be healed, to work miracles."

It all seemed so logical. I had heard

those passages read in church since I was a tiny child. There was always a Scripture reading that accompanied the mass. But it had always bounced off my ears as drops of water slide off duck feathers. Now, however, as our family huddled together, reading, discussing, even beginning to pray, everything was different.

School started in September. Joey, at 13, was back in his usual special education class. I had watched him change that summer. His hyperactivity had diminished and he was entering into our family Bible discussions and prayer times with great enthusiasm. He seemed far more sure of himself than ever before.

I didn't realize how radical the change actually was, though, until I received a call from his special education teacher. It was the week after school began.

"I don't think Joey should be in the special education class this year," she said. "He's changed. I think we should try him in a regular class where he can get into the nitty-gritty of spelling, English, and math."

We made the switch. The end of the

first week of October Joey brought home his first report card. I was in the kitchen when he came in. He looked up, his eyes brimming with joy. His mouth, surrounded by the fading scars, was in a wide grin.

"Guess what, Mom," he said. "I made the honor roll."

He handed me the card and dashed through the kitchen toward the backyard to get his bike. I stood for a long time looking down at the A's and B's on his grade card. The tears filled my eyes, rolled over the edges and streamed down my face. I thought back to that time of desperate prayer in Chicago when I had stripped myself naked before God on behalf of my son, only to think I was rejected. I don't know what I expected back then—a roll of thunder, writing on the wall? It made no difference; God had heard. In quietness and stillness He had heard—and answered. My tears had been my prayer. Healing had been His answer.

I slipped to my knees, hands clutching the report card. "I praise You," I wept. "Oh, how I praise You!"

Several nights later (the days were all jammed together it seemed), I knelt by my bed after the children had been tucked in. It had been a rough day, physically, and my body was exhausted. I was crying. Coming into the presence of the Holy God made me so aware of my unworthiness. Everything I had done wrong seemed to pass before my eyes.

"Forgive me, Lord," I wept. "Really, truly, come into my life."

As I prayed I became aware something was happening inside me, spiritually. It was as though a spring, long covered with stones and leaves, had been un-capped and was now pouring pure water out of my soul. What was that passage Carol had read just the other night? Wasn't it a promise Jesus had made to His followers about the Holy Spirit? Hadn't He said, "Out of your innermost being shall flow rivers of living water"?

That night I slept peacefully. Another verse kept running through my mind as I dozed off, one that Ronnie had read to us several weeks before. "He giveth his beloved sleep."

9. It Happened in Pittsburgh

The next day I called Nell Adams. She had patiently stayed away, had withdrawn her pressure for me to go to another miracle service. She was a very wise woman who knew that the seed which had been planted in Chicago would one day take root, spring up, and bear fruit. At any rate, I felt the harvest season was at hand so I gave her a call.

"You told me Miss Kuhlman conducted miracle services in Pittsburgh on Friday mornings," I said. "Where are they held?"

"In the First Presbyterian Church," she answered, and I could hear the joy bells tinkling in her voice. Her patience and prayers had paid off.

I talked to the children. They all felt as strongly as I did. They didn't even object to driving all the way to Pittsburgh in our old car.

Nell loaned me her copy of Miss Kuhlman's book, *I Believe in Miracles*, so we could know more about this unusual but consistently fruitful ministry. I then bought a copy of *God Can Do It Again*. The more I read, the more I believed God did not want us sick.

We read all the way to Pittsburgh. Carol and Ronnie would take turns reading aloud while I drove. On two occasions even Joey read.

I had not been driving much, and the long trip was really an adventure in faith. I would drive with my left foot on the pedal because my right leg was almost useless. For a month I had been dragging it behind me as I walked. My eyes, too, were giving me real problems, and by the time we reached Pittsburgh we were all exhausted.

We spent the night at a downtown hotel,

just a block from the stately old gray-stone church where the services are con-ducted.

It was still dark at five o'clock the next morning when Carol woke us, shak-ing our beds and pushing us into the bathroom.

"One of us has to be healthy enough to hold a place in line," she said, her eyes sparkling with excitement. "I'm go-ing on down. You all come as soon as possible. God is going to do something special today for all of us." With that she was out of the room.

"Oh, baby," I thought, "I hope you're right."

Ronnie was so sick and weak that morning that Joey and I had to support him down the dark street past the Mellon Square parking garage. The line in front of the building was already two blocks long, extending down toward the heart of town into the cold, gray mist of the early dawn. The city was just coming to life for a new day, and I could not grasp the full impact of seeing all these people waiting in front of the church—waiting for a miracle.

Carol was waving. She had saved us

a place. We stood and stood, crushed, it seemed, by the press of the crowd.

We took turns helping Ronnie stand; but when the doors were opened, we almost lost our grip on him. The surging mob forced us up the steps and literally propelled us down the aisle into the big church.

We found a pew together, about half way down. Moments later we realized the building was full. Every seat taken. Balconies, choir loft behind us, and a huge overflow auditorium in front of us behind the pulpit area—all were packed with people.

Again I was overcome by a desire to praise God. The singing started and I lost myself in it. The crowd, no longer a pushing mob, was welded together into one body through praise.

Fifteen minutes after the singing began (it seemed as if it were seconds) I began to feel heat. It was November, and I of course assumed the heat had been turned on in the building. Yet I grew hotter and hotter—uncomfortably so.

Ronnie was sitting beside me, and during a tiny break in the singing, just as

Miss Kuhlman was coming up to speak, he leaned over and whispered in my ear, "Mom, are you hot? I'm burning up."

"Oh no," I thought. "Surely we're not both going into a crisis right here in the church—at the same time."

I put my hand on Ronnie's forehead. He *felt* cool. I looked at the other people around me. No one seemed to be hot. Some of the women had sweaters draped over their shoulders. But I felt as if I were in a furnace.

Miss Kuhlman was speaking, but the heat was so intense I couldn't listen. I wanted to get out, to get a breath of fresh air, but I felt I needed to stay, unsure of what was going on. Again I tried to concentrate on Miss Kuhlman. She was talking about the Holy Spirit, about miracles. I had come all this way to hear her, but the burning was so intense I could not listen. I felt Carol's hand on my arm.

"Mom, Joey and I are burning up. What's wrong?"

Now I was frightened. What was this? Then, as quickly as I thought it, the heat disappeared. It had been on us for an hour, and now it was gone. Not only did it leave, but I felt a cool breeze wafting across my face, my thighs, all the way down to my feet. It was as though a window had been opened and a fresh breath of cool air was rippling across my body, encasing me in a gentle breeze.

I glanced at Ronnie, then at Joey and Carol. They felt it too. They were grinning in relief.

I turned back to the platform. A lady had been healed of multiple sclerosis and had come to the platform to testify. Then almost interrupting her as she talked, Miss Kuhlman moved quickly to the microphone, her voice ringing with excitement.

"Somebody," she said, her words coming rapidly, "somebody who drags her right leg has been healed. You're seated RIGHT DOWN HERE!" She was pointing directly at me. "Stand up! Claim your healing!"

Nothing, not even a mountain on my shoulders, could have kept me seated. I knew she meant me. I leapt to my feet!

Then I realized my children were

standing too—Ronnie on my right, Carol on my left. All three of us had been healed!

Instantly, it seemed, there was a woman in the aisle leaning over the others and whispering, "Have you been healed?"

"Oh yes!" I sobbed. "We've all been healed. I know it. We've been healed of myasthenia gravis."

There was an audible gasp from the people around us who heard what I said. All around me I could hear people whispering softly, "Praise God! Thank You, Jesus!" A man and a woman in the pew behind me, total strangers, were weeping. The man was so overcome he had his face buried in a handkerchief. A woman in front of us turned and touched my hand, as though she were touching something very sacred, very holy.

I had never felt so much love, so much thanksgiving, so much praise. I felt like a lost child who had been the object of a great search by her family, who had wandered in out of the woods and been caught up in the arms of her father. I looked around. Almost as great a miracle as my healing was the miracle of love. This was my family. These people whom I had never seen before, who were reaching out to me in love, were my real brothers and sisters. And God was my Father. No longer was I bound to an earthly inheritance which passed disease from father to daughter and on to my own children. I had been cut loose and was spiritually joined to another Father—my true Father, a Father from whom I would never inherit death or disease—only life and health. The very genes and chromosomes in my body were being changed as I was adopted into the family of my new Father. And with that transaction came healing and health to my lineage—my children.

Ronnie was the first up the aisle, lifting his legs high as he walked. Only an hour before he could hardly stand. Now he was filled with life—new life.

The three of us waited on the platform for Miss Kuhlman to interview us. Others who had been healed of a variety of diseases were in front of us. But instead of letting us come to the microphone, Miss Kuhlman suddenly turned and headed toward us. No words were spoken. She just pointed in our general direction and said "Oh, the power of God is all over this place."

And we all fell down. I mean all of us: Ronnie, Carol and all the other people standing around us. One second we were waiting in line and the next we were all on the floor. I didn't faint. I wasn't even aware of falling. It was like one of the myasthenia gravis attacks when suddenly the nerves stop transmitting sensations to the muscles and everything stops working for a moment. Whatever it was, it wasn't MG, for this time we were back on our feet. We were refreshed. Then before we knew it, we were back in our seats.

Joey was waiting. His eyes were brimming with tears and he grabbed my hand. "Mother, I can hear! I can hear!"

One of Miss Kuhlman's helpers was back in the aisle. No doubt she had noticed the commotion we were causing. Indeed, no one in our area was paying any attention to what was happening on the platform. They were all watching us as I hugged Joey close to my chest and Carol and Ronnie held on from the outside, crying and laughing.

Then we were all back on the platform again. I explained to Miss Kuhlman about Joey's deafness—total deafness in his left ear, with minimal hearing in his right. The doctors had said there was "no hope, ever" for his hearing. Now he could hear!

Miss Kuhlman checked his hearing and then turned to me. "And you, also, and the other children. All healed of myasthenia gravis. How do you know?"

I explained that I was a nurse, that I was the state coordinator of the MG Foundation. I had my pills in my purse which I was to take every thirty minutes. But it had been four hours and I was feeling wonderful. Instead of going into a crisis, I had been healed.

Miss Kuhlman lifted her hands in praise, and suddenly we were all back on the floor—all four of us this time. We climbed to our feet and fell back again; the power of God was so great. Heaven was outpoured in our midst.

10. How Big Is God?

It was almost three o'clock when we returned to our car and headed toward Louisville. We had missed lunch, but it didn't matter. Our whole family had been healed. Who could think of food at a time like that? And who could think of medicine? We were so filled with the glory of God that there just wasn't any thought of medicine. And we've never taken a pill since.

We arrived home at midnight and Ronnie hit the back door running. When I got into the kitchen, I found him down on his stomach on the floor—doing push-ups.

Medically speaking I knew I was going to need proof. I knew there were remissions in myasthenia gravis, although I had never known of one like this—and certainly not three at the same time. I decided to wait and let God test it out for me.

Three days later the first test came. I caught a severe case of flu. Ordinarily such an attack would have put me in the hospital in a respirator. Yet despite the raging fever and body pains, I remained strong. I recovered in two days and was back on my feet. God's healing was quite complete.

The doctor just shook his head when he examined us. Happy, but noncommittal, he said none of us was any longer showing symptoms of myasthenia gravis.

I didn't expect him to testify to our miracle. I would do that. Simply confirming that all the symptoms were gone—for all of us—was enough for me.

The final test of my healing came a year later. I was having some severe female bleeding and my gynecologist insisted I have an immediate operation. He did not know of my healing from myasthenia gravis and expressed great concern that I would have to go under anesthesia, which is the ultimate test for a myasthenic. Very few advanced cases come out of surgery alive. I drove myself to the hospital, signed myself in, and went into surgery alone. The operating room was ready for me, equipped with respirator and all the necessary drugs to bring me back to life in case my lungs stopped while I was on the operating table. But God had breathed health into me. I was safe.

I spent the pre-op time witnessing to a nun, one of the scrub nurses who had known me for a long time. I came out of the recovery room much faster than an ordinary person, got up the next morning and drove myself home.

I said to my amazed doctor, "God did this just to show all these medical people whom I have known so long that I have been healed."

He looked at me and grinned. "Indeed you have," he said with a farewell pat on my shoulder. "Indeed you have."

I know that physical healing should never be seen as an end in itself. I believe God heals our bodies to bring us to a far greater end than physical health —that of glorifying Him. This has been demonstrated in my life and the lives of my three children many times over.

For his thirteenth birthday Joey expressed the wish that the best birthday present he could receive would be to feel as close to Jesus as he had felt His presence at a Kathryn Kuhlman service. Our friends gathered with us that day and gave praise to the Father for the miracles He had given us. Joey was filled with the Spirit as Carol and Ronnie had been before him. We knew, then, that this was just one of many wonderful encounters we would have with our blessed Savior!

I still cling to my Roman Catholic identity, but I now see far beyond the walls of my own group to that *greater* thing God is doing in the world—bringing His Body together so it will be prepared to receive His Son when He returns.

As great as my healing has been, as grateful as I am for the touch of God on the bodies of my children, far greater is the wonderful assurance that I am part of His Bride, awaiting the soon coming of the King.

As a nurse, as a teacher of nurses, my healing does not make me believe any less in medicine. In fact, it has helped me understand the entire healing process much better. I see doctors, nurses, hospitals and drugs as a part of God's great healing process. But I also see beyond— to a loving heavenly Father who longs to restore the gift of miracles, the gifts of healing, to the Church.

There will always be a need for doctors and nurses. The greatest book on miracles—the book of Acts—was written by a physician, Dr. Luke. Yet I now understand there is more, far more, than those of us who have spent our lives in medical science can comprehend with the mind. This "far more" is the power of the Holy Spirit. And no one is more grateful than I am—than we are—that God is restoring this power to His people.

I am still active with the Myasthenia Gravis Foundation. Only now, as I travel the state informing MG patients and their families about the disease, I bring them something I was never able to give before. Hope!

Incurable? Hopeless? These words have been crossed out of my medical vocabulary. I have four living affidavits to attest to the power of God to do the impossible: Carol, Joey, Ronnie and myself.

How big is God?

BIG ENOUGH!